Ozark Crows

Carolyn Guinzio

SPUYTEN DUYVIL

New York City

Library of Congress Cataloging-in-Publication Data

Names: Guinzio, Carolyn, author.
Title: Ozark crows / Carolyn Guinzio.
Description: New York City : Spuyten Duyvil, 2018.
Identifiers: LCCN 2017055093| ISBN 9781947980228
Classification: LCC PS3607.U5426 A6 2018 | DDC 813/.6--dc23
LC record available at https://lccn.loc.gov/2017055093

for Warren and Charlotte
and
for Davis

CONTENTS

The sky
The balance
The fall
The mind
The b(r)ead
The heart
The mobbing
The silence
The hour
The murder
The field
The frost
The winter
The ribbon
The throat
The orbs
The echo
The sliver
The reach
The sound
The branches
The dusk
The road
The dream
The cache
The funeral

NOTES

I was alone when

I left the frame

I entered the frame

I was alone when

If you could drag the things of childhood forward through your life

I feel it shifting under my feet in the bumps on the branches

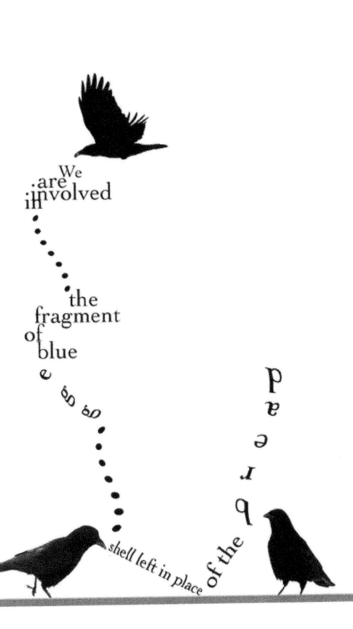

We
are
in involved

the
fragment
of blue
e
g g
e
shell left in place of the

bread

The sky is nothing but a blank until we draw our lines across it

The sky is nothing but a blank until we draw our lines across it

The sky is nothing but a blank until we draw our lines across it

The sky is nothing but a blank until we draw our voices across it

The sky is nothing but a blank until we draw our voices across it

The sky is nothing but a blank until we draw our voices across it

The sky is nothing but a blank until we draw our voices across it

We are not harbingers

We like to talk

About what we can see

From the sky

The infinite

in ninety sounds

is contained

The map is covered with pins · The wing is a map · Silences are pinned to the wing · The map is covered with pins ... The wing is a map ... Silences are pinned to the wing

In the second before it fell

our hearts fluttered open and dark

crashing with the branches

to the the ground

If you would learn our language

We would tell you what we know

We would tell you what we know

If you would learn our language

The night used to be dark —

The first flickering, the unseeable —

We waited and waited when night was night —

Mercury is slipping off the side of the sky —

THE STORM

What keeps you from falling over the edge of the sky

When we are quiet it means a storm

When we are loud it means a storm

The cone of the cone flower has a pattern that also occurs in the sky

THE THOUGHTS

to the sky?

from the ground

What chases us down from the sky

and up

They are nothing but dreams

to the ground

The trees draw lines in the sky
Our shadows circle the tree
Darkness hides in itself

THE WIND

We watch the vulture to learn what it learns from the wind

The signal was a dime-sized piece of glass that could be seen from the sky in the sun glittering

We drink

the rain

that slides

down the remnants

of the ancient range

We wait silent and open-

mouthed

on the radiating waves

over your head

We waited at the edge of the water until the water was gone

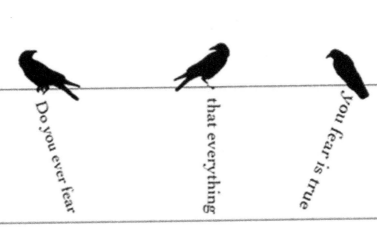

Do you ever fear

that everything

you fear is true

is true

THE CORNER

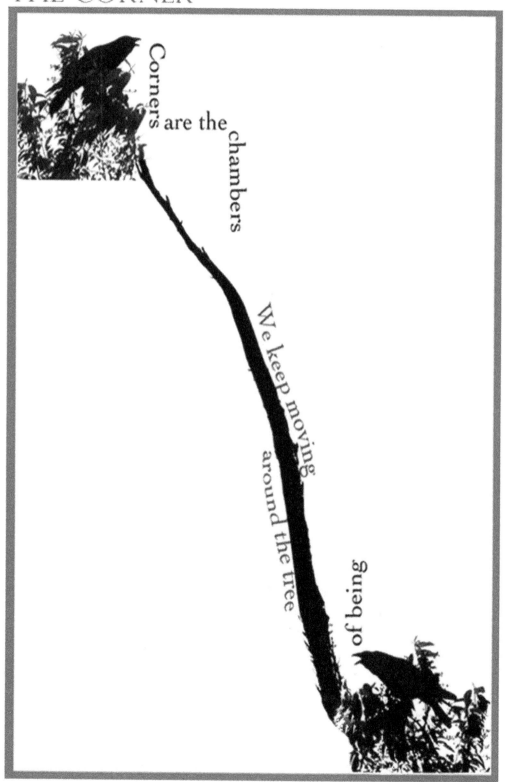

Corners are the chambers

We keep moving around the tree of being

The elements are arguing over what

over what

we........should........become

become

THE WINDOW

What's the darkest truth you ever heard?

A pane placed between not space but time.

We can't see that far.

What is a window of time?

when we thought us to explain it to Yourself we were alone during You should stop trying Remember the morning overhead us

When our tools are not enough we turn to yours

They think we can see the future

Can you see the future?

I thought you were moving toward me but you were actually flying away

We placed a cicada **husk** to remember beneath this tree

a soundless presence behind it

we are the first thing

when it burns off in the morning

that comes back into being

THE SNOW

The snow is erasing our path through as we fly the sky

THE WATER

We are not real

We are not in the tree

we are in the water

Are we in the tree?
We are reflections

We are not falling
We are real

We are not falling
Are we real?

We are in the tree
Our shadows are falling

We are not in the water

Are we falling?

The rain is falling

Are we real?

Fragments of the self

are forever drifting down

to the ground

THE PATH

Where are you going alone in the wide world?

With all understand the word alone

I shall take the straightest path to be with you

There is much in the word alone

I can almost reach it

The satellite is swinging around

The moon is looking up from the pools in the ground

I can almost reach it

THE ETHER

Three times I heard a plane and looked up when my eye fell instead upon you you you you you you you you you you you you you you you you you you you you you you you you you you you you you you you

The lines in the earth are deeper and great

They lead to the end of the day

The world doesn't end

The world ends in a line of trees

THE CLOUDS

Something is going to happen today

finally

Have you read the clouds?

The sky is a page. There is a sen se of movement across it.

Yes, we stole the egg

No thing is alone in this of the sparrow

kind of sorrow

steals the egg of the crow

The raccoon

We will need each other
to guard against
the future
Stand close to me

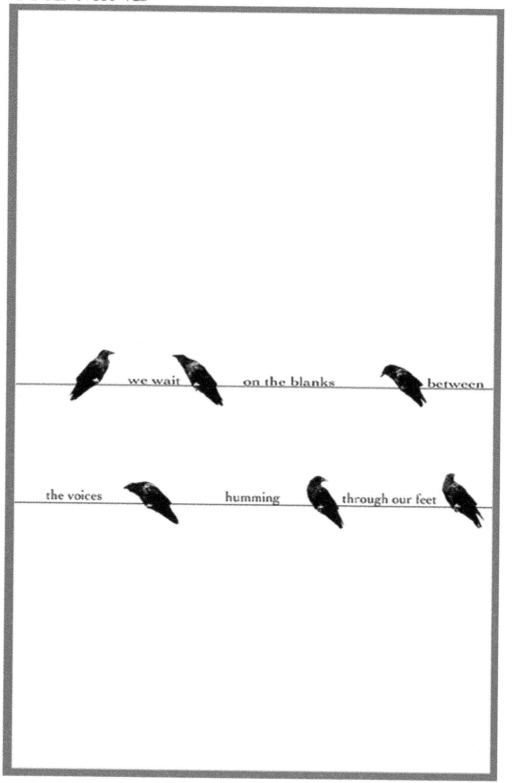

we wait   on the blanks   between

the voices   humming   through our feet

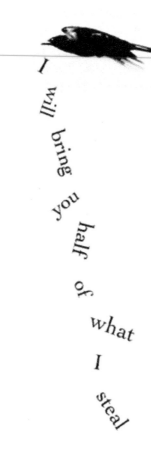

I will bring you half of what I steal

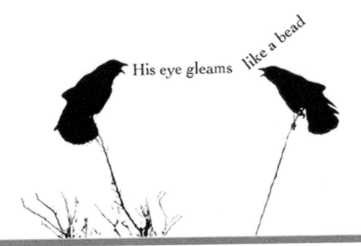

His eye gleams like a bead

THE HEART

I am bringing my pink- mouthed fledgings back to the first trees that I knew

Our quietness means

we see you

below us in the grass

Time is marked by lines in the sky we feel with our feet

They call our minds criminal

They call our crowds crimes

We carry the weight of our ancestors

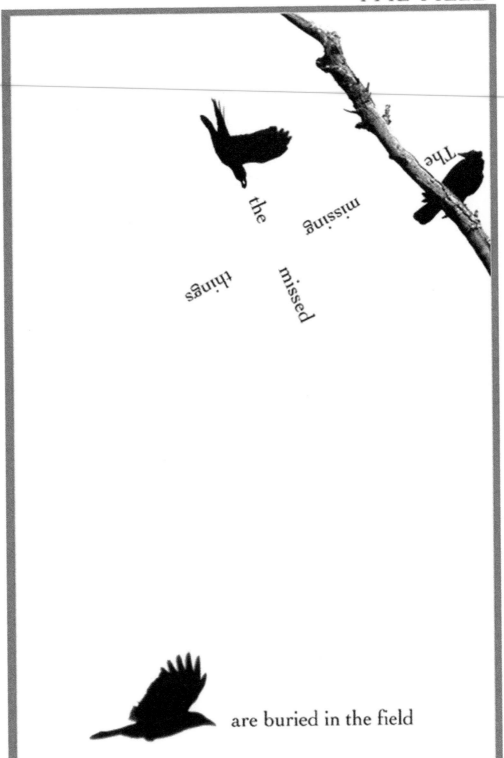

The
the
missing
things
missed

are buried in the field

THE FROST

The breath of our phantom ancestors is hovering in the atmosphere It will come to rest in the grass

We keep looking for a place that will make us invisible

We let the frost from the root
that burst from the root
melt on our tongues

A sound crossing the sky like the shadow of a string

I can still call to you when it's closed

One of them stays the same. One of them is always changing.

I want your voice
not my own
calling out of the bluff

I want your voice
not my own
calling out of the bluff

THE SLIVER

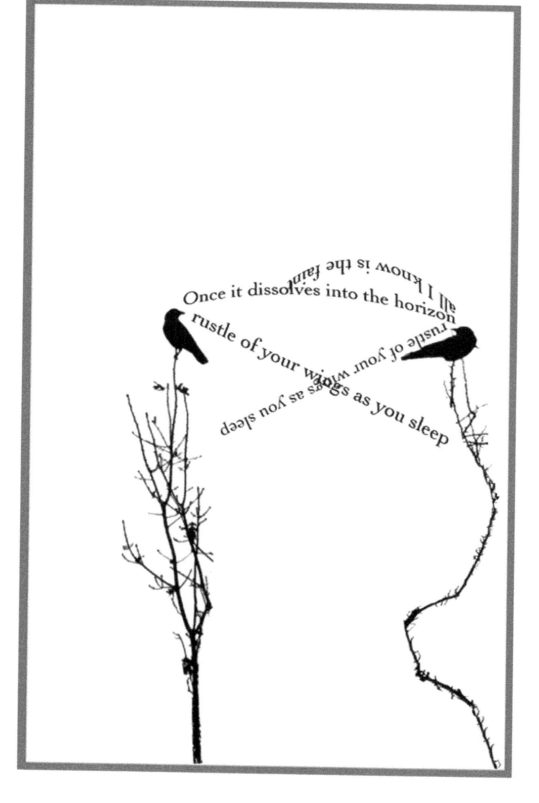

Once it dissolves into the horizon
all I know is the faint
rustle of your wings as you sleep

THE SOUND

I've called you by the same sound since the nest

I've called you by the same sound since the nest

That's how we know it's you

That's how we know it's you

Will I always be alone?

You will not be alone

You will not be alone

You will not be alone

The branches are saying silence

We begin again in the morning

The horizon is saying absence

Only when we feel your breath beginning to push past will we move into the margin

THE DREAM

Sometimes at night there is a wind that tosses about our minds instead of feathers

Though our mouths

turned from

have

black

pink to

we remember everything

I will know you. I will know you. I will know you. I will know you.

I will know you.

Wild things die knowing only themselves?

I will know you.

I will know you. I will know you.

NOTES

This project came about after years of observation and interaction with crows, particularly the family photographed for the poems. All the images are original, taken in the Arkansas Ozark Mountains. There are instances where source material was consulted and where literature inspired, including *The American Crow and the Common Raven* by Lawrence Kilhan (Texas A&M, 1989), *Bird Brains* by Candace Savage (Sierra Club Books, 1995) and *The Snow Queen* by Hans Christian Anderson. Thank you to Spuyten Duyvil Press for their generosity in bringing this book into being.

My gratitude to the editors of the journals where the following pieces appeared. A video podcast about the book appeared on the Authors Talk Series at Superstition Review.

THE ECHO
THE SLIVER   ABOUT PLACE
THE FUNERAL
THE ILLUSION

THE ELEMENTS
THE TRANSLATION   BOSTON REVIEW
THE TRIAL
THE WATER

THE DAWN
THE GLASS
THE HORIZON   DIAGRAM
THE NEST
THE MIND

THE B(R)EAD
THE HEART
THE HOUR   DIODE
THE MURDER
THE SILENCE

Carolyn Guinzio is the author of four previous collections including *Spoke & Dark*, winner of the To The Lighthouse/A Room Of Her Own Prize. Her work has appeared in Agni, Bomb, The New Yorker, and many other journals. A Chicago native, she has lived in the Arkansas Ozarks since 2002 with her husband, the poet Davis McCombs, and their two children Warren and Charlotte. Her website is carolynguinzio.tumblr.com

Printed in November 2021
by Rotomail Italia S.p.A., Vignate (MI) - Italy